ZAHA HADID ARCHITECTS
HEYDAR ALIYEV CENTER

ZAHA HADID ARCHITECTS
HEYDAR ALIYEV CENTER

Edited by Saffet Kaya Bekiroglu

Lars Müller Publishers

CONTENTS

Abstract, liquid, and incandescent in the sun, the Heydar Aliyev Center in Baku does not look as though it was actually constructed, but seems instead to have appeared, like an emanation, after a magician rubbed a lamp. A landmark in architectural history and engineering, and the new symbol of a new nation, the Center, with a roof that flows into walls that pour onto the ground, tents a national museum, gallery, and auditorium. The design marks a convergence of architectural vision, computational intelligence, and extreme engineering that combine to make the virtuosity of the structure look serene and effortless. With compound curves evolving and revolving inside and out into other curves and countercurves, the surfaces of the free-form structure are as continuous as a Möbius strip or Klein bottle. Like venerable cathedrals and mosques, the Center holds a mystifying aura that conditions visitors for the experiences inside.

FAST FORWARD

Joseph Giovannini

In his brilliant disquisitions on the geometry of power, French *philosophe* Michel Foucault discussed panopticons, nineteenth-century prisons designed with corridors radiating like spokes from a hub that gave guards visual control over prisoners. But for a contemporary example of how architecture spatializes power, Foucault might have just boarded a plane to the then Soviet republic of Azerbaijan where the imposing, classically detailed Government House in Baku still commands a downtown neighborhood through its unyielding geometry. Sited at a pivotal and central intersection, isolated in its unforgiving, virtually fortified relationship with the surrounding city, the symmetrical, layer-cake, four-poster structure is almost a caricature of the period's communism. Designed in 1934 and finished in 1952, the stern, rigid, unavoidable structure is unyielding in its control over both the neighborhood and its own architectural strata and parts; each element in the classical ordination cemented in its place without question or exception. Surrounding streets and plazas obey a stern order as visualized in the geometries of the building and reified in its mass.

That was then. The Soviet Union dissolved, Azerbaijan became independent, and twenty years on, Baku has built a new symbol of the state, the Heydar Aliyev Center. Government House still exists, but it has been superseded by an antimonumental monument, devoted to culture rather than government, with an architecture that sheds the geometry of power in favor of a geometry of freedom. The 260 ft. tall [80 meters], 600,000-square-foot [57,000 square meters] free-form building, flowing like lava from mountainous peaks, embodies not rigidity, but fluidity, with curving shapes and spaces and scalloped edges that spill into the surrounding park and flow into interiors that rise, turn, and fall through apparently endless valleys and caverns, no visual terminus in sight.

Paradigms have shifted in the architecture of the capital. Instead of spatializing power, the Center spatializes freedoms.

With undulating edges hovering over walls of glass looking inside onto intimations of white infinities, the architectural attitude of the Center is open, transparent, and democratic. There is no secretive wall around the park in which it sits. The building and its grounds belong to the public, not to a bureaucracy housed in a closed box. With gestural shapes that might belong to a sculpture in the museum, the building is a gift to the street and the public.

Many famous architects are called by cities and countries to create new icons that will stand as symbols of culture and social progress. In a globalized cultural economy, with cities competing for visibility and status, architects have become agents of image and civic branding. But few deliver as regularly and spectacularly as Zaha Hadid, and her successes over the last decade—in rapid succession, the MAXXI museum in Rome, the Guangzhou Opera House in China, the Broad Art Museum at Michigan State University, the Glasgow Riverside Museum of Transport— are so consistent that her methodology and theories must be acknowledged and credited. Their IQ cannot simply be attributed to strokes of inspiration delivered late at night by divine afflatus. Dame Zaha Hadid knows what she's doing. There is method to the practice, and principle. She has led one of the most consistently inventive offices anywhere for more than thirty years.

She does not write manifestos. She builds them. Theory is inscribed implicitly in her designs, and a careful reading of the Center as built yields an understanding that the quest for beauty alone is not her modus operandi. The building is beautiful, even exquisitely beautiful, and beauty may account for its strong and seductive urban presence, for its hold on the eye. But beauty does not account for its importance. Nor does the virtuosity in its sea of structurally difficult compound curves.

Designed by Hadid, with her associate Patrik Schumacher and project architect Saffet Kaya Bekiroglu, the building is not simply formalist. The beauty and virtuosity of the Heydar Alivev Center are married to meaning. The architecture breaks social ground with its democratic attitude, offering generous expanses of articulated public space inside and out. The promenades in the surrounding park and into and through the building urbanize the environment, making it accessible and civic, while inviting exploration. The acts of peripatetic participation it elicits foster a sense of personal ownership. With multiple ground planes and sectional interconnectivity, its open form and spatial porosity stand as analogs for openness in cultural and political systems. Form and space are relational rather than absolute. The dynamic becoming of its curves implies change, rather than stasis, as an existential condition, the result of a design process based in factoring flux into the design equation rather than axiomatic rules.

And then there is the raw physics of its inspiring spaces. Its success as a symbol is not a result of size and bombast, but its power "to stir mens' blood," as Chicago city planner Daniel Burnham said about making "no little plans." Its spectacle is not hollow but activist, engaging the senses and inciting the imagination. The building is an object with great subjective appeal.

The clients asked for a national culture center that would contain galleries, a museum and 1,000-seat conference center auditorium on a large parcel of land in a part of Baku just outside the main city. But the clients wanted more than a vessel filled with functions. As much for their own citizens as for audiences abroad, they wanted an aspirational building that would symbolize the progressive nature of the nation and its emerging status as a first-world country with a robust economy and visible achievements. Like Frank Gehry's Bilbao, or Hadid's own Guangzhou Opera House, the building would be a destination on the international culture map now being redrawn through ambitious, image-oriented architectural projects, new "temples" with an international call.

The commission was not about transforming quaint and exotic local symbols of a romanticized and orientalized past, but about a culture striving for modernity, and for recognition on the world stage. The building could be a wand helping to catalyze a prominence that Azerbaijan has worked hard to deserve. Imagery mattered: the clients wanted a building for export that would appeal as much on a computer screen, a magazine cover, or a stamp, as it does on the site.

The nearly 14-acre parcel of land was previously occupied by an abandoned Soviet-era factory, and isolated by wide thoroughfares beyond which lay districts of bland apartment blocks with little urban cohesion. Effectively, there was little context; or rather there was no context worth reacting to and building on. The architects had to invent a new context in a desolate tabula rasa.

Ever since The Peak, Hadid's 1983 breakout project for a sports club in the heights above Hong Kong, she has been interested in the reciprocal relationship of building and site. The floors of the club exploded from the hillside like a spray of crystal quartz even as they imploded, architecturalizing the surrounding ground. In this and later projects, Hadid has consistently brought the outside into her buildings, and the inside out, in an effort to cultivate and sustain public space on either side of the front door. In Baku, she was able to work at a scale and with a scope that afforded wide berth to her ambitions of creating public space. Hadid, perhaps influenced by the politics of her father, a progressive politician in Iraq during its democratic period, has always cultivated public space in her designs to democratize the buildings. And she often extends the street life into the interiors.

The size of ten football fields, the parcel was a large enough canvas for Hadid to test architecture-cum-urban design with the theses she has been developing for decades—especially her interest in developing object and field, figure and ground, as reciprocal functions of each other.

Since postmodernism, contextual design in architecture has typically meant matching cornice lines. But Hadid's interpretation of context starts at the ground. She does not think of the ground as a tea tray on which to place a samovar. Land is not simply ground for a sculptural figure. Context for Hadid is a diagram of tangible and intangible influences swarming a site like a Jackson Pollock painting, an energy field that basically pushes and pulls the building dynamically into a reiterative play of form, space, and function.

Like a water witch wielding a divining rod, she dowses for points of pressure and relaxation, ebb and flow, designing simultaneously in plan, section, and elevation buildings without predetermined shape. She does not think planimetrically but instead has long studied buildings as X-rays of spatial bodies moving dynamically through space. Her use of the computer over the last twenty years, with the on-screen transparency of lines, has confirmed the process, as has the advent of parametric programs used to develop designs dynamically in a changing flow of influence and input.

So Hadid and her associates do not start with Platonic primitives, or any closed form, but escape the fixity of regular geometries that, like Baku's Government House, pin, wall, and otherwise control space. Form for Zaha Hadid Architects is mutable rather than absolute, susceptible to interpretation and change. The implications of open architectural form are pregnant with social and political corollaries, including the suggestion of open societies. In the context of ex-Soviet Baku, especially with the precedent of Government House, the Center sets a promising precedent and hopeful direction.

In Baku the long site had a rise of about 20 meters, enough to suggest an elongated propylea up to an acropolis. The architects mapped the path and provoked Hitchcockian suspense by designing a geometrically intricate delta of terraced pools, fed by banks of cascading water traversed by straight paths and zigzag switchbacks. A large food and restaurant pavilion, with a slanting roof and walls that emerge out of the topology of the sloping site, activates the lower end of the park. A subway will soon be extended to the foot of the esplanade. The waterfalls and pools emphasize the fluid nature of the entire vision, contrasting with the conventional apartment blocks, many dour, which surround it.

The complex geometries of paths, pools, and program architecturalize the park, which crests at the high end atop a large, stepped underground parking lot. The urban landscape grows out of a sectional design strategy of terraces. Pedestrians who have strolled up the paths gather with visitors who have parked, and together they converge on a sprawling plaza in front of the Center. The complexity recalls Hadid's design of layered geometries and activities, which she proposed in her 1983 entry for the Parc de la Villette competition in Paris.

Every geometry in the park moves, always on the way to, and becoming, something else. There are no fixed points, no spatial moments suitable, for example, for an obelisk. Hadid never pins space. The entire topography, including the site and the building, is fluid. The white concrete plane of the plaza at the top plateau beyond the parking lot lifts, peeling up into curved surfaces that flow forward into a free-form shell that swells, splits, and rises in contours between two peaks, before flowing and cascading down again into the white, abstract ground plane. Edges undulate like cruising stingrays. The building exhibits no sense of weight, only lift.

For Hadid, the blur between field and object is fundamental. The object emerges within the field, and the field grows from the object. The building is an eruptive moment in the larger topology, an intensification of the field heaving up into a "shell" that climaxes here in an 80-meter roof that peaks over the nine levels within. The shell, a free-form space truss with folds, gaps, and gills that pour natural light inside, fuses the three institutions beneath into a seamless figure that is contemporary and abstract but mystifying.

For Le Corbusier, the plan was the generator, but for Hadid, a three-dimensional force field, stereometric rather than planimetric, was the generator of a design conceived simultaneously as plan, section, and elevation. Gravity in this omnidirectional vision is no longer privileged and dominant but suspended and aqueous.

The building is so unusual by any historic frame of reference that in Baku, along the trunk road between the airport and town, it has a talismanic presence: even taxi drivers regularly turn their heads as they pass to look. The building doesn't dominate, casting visitors in a submissive role, but elicits curiosity.

Some buildings are question marks that must be explored to be understood. Visitors step into the embrace of the building where two wings wrap a forecourt and usher them through a tall, wide wall of glass into a cavernous foyer. Having architecturalized the outdoor space into a built landscape, the architects extend the urbanism of the exterior inside by flowing the public spaces into a foyer that spreads dramatically as it soars vertically. The architects have grouped the library, museum, and conference auditorium, along with a banquet area, in this decentralized, flowing atrium. The space can handle separate events at the same time.

Conceived outside and inside as a continuous surface, the building starts with white floors that become white walls that become white ceilings in contoured shapes that erase any thought of cardinal directions or Cartesian coordination. There is a sense of ceremony even without ceremonies. Influenced by the Russian avant-garde, who conceived public spaces as "urban condensers" catalyzing a public realm of activity, Hadid has always cultivated the civics of public space. Here the sheer white grandeur of the processional promenade rivals even the operatic staircases of the Paris Opéra. As in Paris, its majesty celebrates public gathering and movement. In an age when one architect often does the shell and another the interior, the Center has the distinction of achieving full stature as an interior, as a function of the commission but also as a matter of principle: exterior and interior surfaces are related and continuous.

Space is a slippery medium difficult to identify, conceive, and design when unboxed. Instead of making public space in the French and Italian tradition of surrounding an open area with buildings, or walling it like a conventional room, Hadid layers space three-dimensionally to create voids. The public space inside the Center is truly omnidirectional, flowing laterally and vertically in vistas that bend with the curves.

Each program element looks different because of its height requirements and function. The floors at the back, stacked nine stories high, house the library, and the closed volumes to the right contain the auditorium of the conference center, surrounded by a curving foyer with an outer wall billowing like a sail. The functions do not stand apart but merge into a dynamic whole, perhaps best described in musical terms such as *glissando* and *crescendo*. The building is really a gerund, always in a state of becoming—floors becoming walls, steps turning into cliffs, the outside diving inside, the ceilings sailing off. The gills and cuts in the exterior surfaces, like Lucio Fontana paintings, allow natural light to feather the interior walls in gentle washes.

The building keeps on giving at every turn, and the masterpiece within the masterpiece is the auditorium, paneled in an oak that imparts a mellow look to the hall, like the burnished glow of a cello. The architects have laminated the ceilings and floors with strips of oak, leaving gaps for lighting between the striations that circle the hall, ceiling to floor. The strips waver like a flame, perhaps a reference to the cult of fire associated with Azerbaijan's native Zoroastrianism. In ancient times, oil seeping to the surface of the ground combusted spontaneously.

Like a Baroque building in Italy, this is a building in movement and self-transformation, always migrating somewhere else, an urban carpet leading visitors onward, ushering them toward new spaces and vistas. The organizational principle is not the box but the stream. Liquid spaces, with a generative assist from computer programs, may be the new space of the new century, and the Heydar Aliyev Center introduces such space in a convincing argument. The atrium expands uninterrupted, with no sense of an end, the continuous surfaces forming a total surround of pure white space. Like a bath, the building is immersive, and experiential, involving visitors by inviting circumnavigation and a participatory relationship. Visitors find themselves in a curving wonderland that widens and narrows, rises and falls, pushing them along in a dynamic flow of converging and diverging walls and ceilings that transmit the dynamism of the shell to the interior.

The design in many ways takes up the direction so brilliantly established by Eero Saarinen, with his segmented shell structure at the TWA Terminal at JFK Airport in New York; a direction truncated by Saarinen's untimely death, and by the choirs of academic critics who misunderstood its subjectivity as an abrogation of modernism's rationalist character. But TWA was the not-Seagram—intentionally. It represented a different direction for a different generation. Saarinen was eschewing technical, rationalist space for "felt" space. Forms engaged the senses and mind through what has been called a "psychophysical spatial immersion." The body empathized with the form. Hadid carries forward and develops this repressed tradition a half century later in a spectacular design whose shells and immersive experience are reinterpreted in another material and technology. The country, time, and culture—that is, the zeitgeist—may be different, but the body and the body's reaction to fluid, continuous, vaulting form remains constant.

The optically rich interior is to some degree a built essay in multiperspectivalism. Multiple vanishing points engage perception so that the space becomes personal, owned by the visitor on a path of physical exploration. Mathematicians might compare its continuous topological surface to the geometries of a Möbius strip or Klein bottle. But off the page, outside the textbook, experientially, curves turning against curves engage the body by capturing the eye, producing a hypnotic effect.

For all the mystification of the forms, the building is clearly organized and easily navigable, with a path running through and around the ground floor, connecting to a staircase rising to galleries and mezzanines above, a vision as light and celestial as a Tiepolo skyscape.

To be wonderful, a wonderland cannot look strained, and the genius of the design is that the architects and engineers maintain the visual levity throughout, with no lapse in tone. The purity of an all-white space would be immediately compromised by visible ducts, grills, and knobs: the architects suppress pesky constructive bumps in support of smooth, clean surfaces that defer to the effect of a weightless shell floating in space without apparent support. In a building of such apparent simplicity and balletic grace, trivial incidents of construction would diminish its effect, and architects and builders took special care detailing the skin so there is nothing to stop the eye from skimming the surfaces. As a practical matter, the 3-meter-high cavity of the shell also accommodates and hides many of the building systems, including lighting and ventilation, accessed by catwalks fitted within the depth of the frame. There were no such cavities in postwar shell buildings such as the TWA Terminal at JFK, which were built in concrete as single shells. In any event, they were not free-form.

Had Hadid revealed the nuts and bolts, she would have lost the flying-carpet effect of a magically supported structure. Although there is no effort at representation, there's a whiff of Turkic tradition, perhaps because of the peaked and cushioned shapes outside. Somehow the free-form shell seems at home in a culture that values sensuousness. But the inference, if any, is oblique, and without a trace of condescending orientalism.

The architects used three-dimensional modeling to shape the shell, along with other two-dimensional documentation. Although Hadid says that she always conceives her projects by drawing, the architects developed the project further with a combination of computer programs. The initial assumption was that the building would be structured with a combination of steel trusses and beams, but early in the construction phase, the builders adopted a free-form space frame engineered and manufactured in Germany, which could elegantly structure the compound curves while minimizing the amount of steel.

Bucky Fuller liked to ask how much a building weighs. The space frame weighed a fraction of the weight of a more conventional steel structure. The manufacturer also shipped the structure to Baku in crates for assembly, much like a piece of IKEA furniture.

The space frame enabled the vision, and the vision encouraged the development of the technology itself, in a symbiotic relationship that resulted in a highly advanced structure and a new precedent. Large and complex asymmetrical shells of this conceptual and technical scope have rarely, if ever, been attempted, even by ZHA. Although the space frame itself is not visible, the design takes advantage of its structural agility in daring moments, such as at the front plaza where the shell dives to the ground in a Nureyev turn, alighting *en pointe*, tons of weight bearing on a toe. Grace under pressure.

Though heroic as structure, the design itself does not privilege structure as a subject or a leading issue. Nowhere is its musculature or skeleton on display. In a reversal of modernism's traditional priorities, skin sets the agenda rather than structure, shifting the building from a static to a visually dynamic reading.

As early as The Peak, Hadid's vision had anticipated the computer, so when it arrived in her office full force in the early 1990s, her vision dovetailed with the new algorithms. Over the last two decades, the computer has been completely absorbed in her practice with a noticeable impact, the sharp angularity of her early work giving way to smooth shapes: The disconnected shards of The Peak, which behaved like filings in a field of forces, in Baku merged into a field of flows, into smooth rather than broken continuums of form and space. The force fields became flow fields. Inspired by the early-twentieth-century paintings of Malevich, Hadid had always painted her structures floating weightlessly against the infinity of white or black backgrounds, without apparent substance: air had always been her medium. With the paradigm shift to the fluid forms encouraged by computer programs, however, water became equally privileged: form and space virtually liquefied as she visualized and developed buildings on screen. The computer was a tool that helped her treat space as a medium transmitting force and warping form within the distortional fields painted by the Russian suprematists. The Baku center belongs to a series of recently developed shell projects that include the Aquatics Center for the 2012 London Olympics.

A masterpiece would seem to be a masterpiece, an absolute without degrees of excellence. But in the unusual case of Zaha Hadid Architects, which produces architectural masterpieces with alarming regularity, there are masterpieces, better masterpieces and best masterpieces. Just when you thought the designs couldn't get more masterful than the MAXXI in Rome, Guangzhou Opera House in China, and the jewel-like Broad Art Museum at Michigan State University, with its fractal forms, the architects produced the Heydar Aliyev Center—lyrical, unexpected, buoyant. Like most of Hadid's buildings, the Center is both delicate and robust, refined and powerful, but the structure surpasses the ambitions of other projects the office has done so far. It is more polished materially, more inventive structurally, more sophisticated technologically, more complex spatially and formally—and generally more resolved and daring.

From the point of view of a city, country, and culture in need of a synoptic symbol, the Center goes beyond program to play an iconic role, one of architecture's most treacherous missions: the wrong architectural gesture can mean embarrassing failure in public. Clients often commission a building they hope will embody civic pride and even national aspirations, but they take a risk. Often well-intended civic and national goals do not find successful architectural form, but in Baku ZHA has produced a national symbol that proves the architectural theses she has been developing for decades. The building also represents, like Frank Lloyd Wright's and Frank Gehry's two Guggenheims, the case of an institution defined by the building that houses it.

As it opens, the building promises to take its place in architectural history as a signal event, momentous for its virtuosic construction, its architectural ideology, and its sheer presence. But the building, despite its scope and sweep, also posits a notable, more local historical irony. Hadid was influenced early on by the Russian avant-garde, especially the suprematists, whose unconsummated work she championed. She set out to build their revolution, which was aborted by the more conservative governments of Lenin and then Stalin, who thought that solid, stolid, classicist, statist structures better represented the ideals of the country they wanted to shape. In the 1920s and '30s, the ranks of the suprematists thinned, and their visions remained unbuilt.

The local irony is that the arguments that once raged in Moscow and St. Petersberg should resume many decades later, and thousands of miles away, in Baku. Stalinist architecture survived in Baku as a strong, unavoidable presence in buildings like Government House even after Azerbaijan achieved independence. But with her design for the Center, Hadid has reengaged the debate, and this time reversed the fortunes of the avant-garde vision. Unlike the Soviet-era buildings—heavy, imposing, dour, implacable—the Center represents a new era in architecture that symbolizes a different Azerbaijan.

If a culture can be extrapolated from the architectural posture represented by the Heydar Aliyev Center, it would be freer and more spirited, and applied with a light touch as well as principled discipline. The Center, an embodiment of an enlightened philosophical framework, is by far more poetic, compelling, and charismatic than its Soviet equivalent down the road. Its open forms promise to help open Azeri culture by an act of attraction rather than imposition. Hadid has designed and crafted an object lesson and a parable.

Azerbaijan commissioned a building, and Hadid met the program. But she also read between the lines and exceeded the brief by delivering a futuristic vision, aspirational ideal, and a defining symbol for the country.

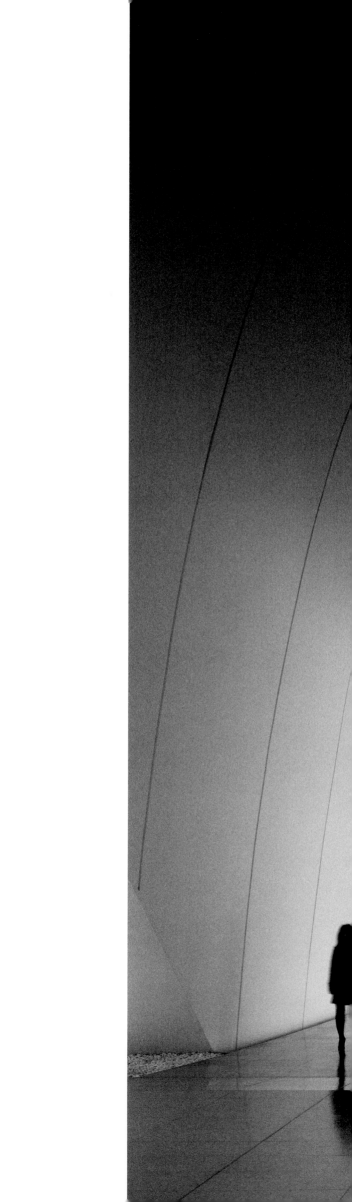

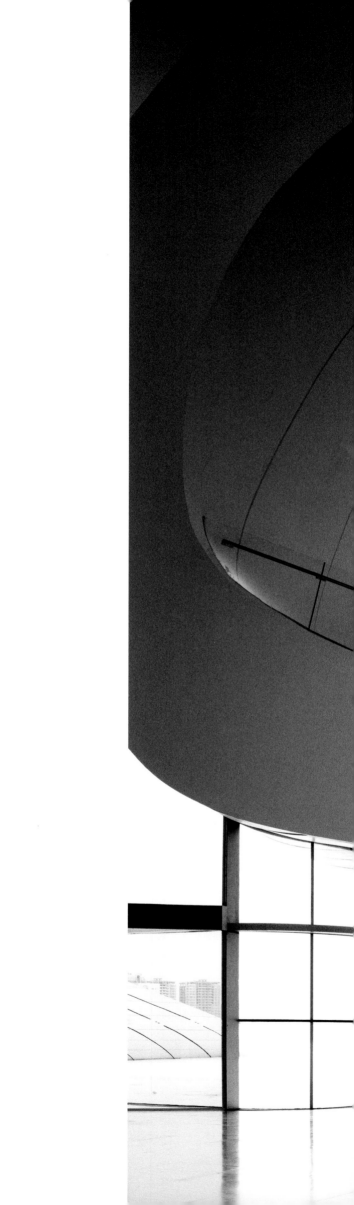

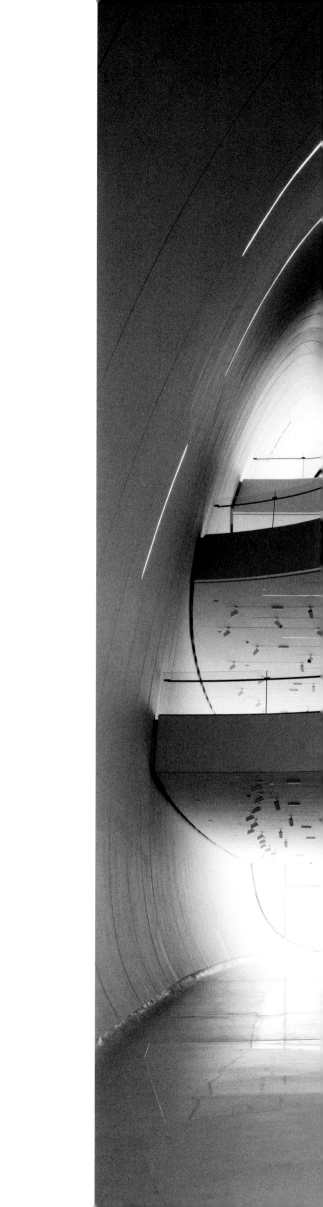

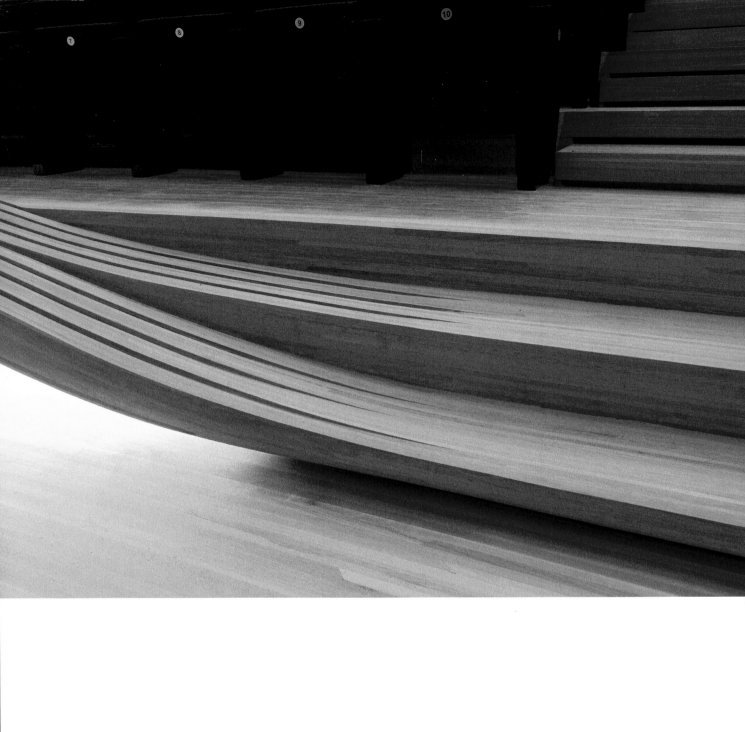

HEYDAR ALIYEV CENTER

Saffet Kaya Bekiroglu, Project Architect, Zaha Hadid Architects

As part of the former Soviet Union, the urbanism and architecture of Baku, the capital of Azerbaijan on the Western coast of the Caspian Sea, was heavily influenced by the planning of that era. Since its independence in 1991, Azerbaijan has invested heavily in modernizing and developing Baku's infrastructure and architecture, departing from its legacy of normative modernism.

Zaha Hadid Architects was appointed as design architects of the Heydar Aliyev Center following a competition in 2007. The Center, designed to become the primary building for the nation's cultural programs, breaks from the rigid and often monumental Soviet architecture that is so prevalent in Baku, aspiring instead to express the sensibilities of Azeri culture and the optimism of a nation that looks to the future.

DESIGN CONCEPT

The design of the Heydar Aliyev Center establishes a continuous, fluid relationship between its surrounding plaza and the building's interior. The plaza as the ground surface, accessible to all as part of Baku's urban fabric, rises to envelop an equally public interior space and define a sequence of event spaces dedicated to the collective celebration of contemporary and traditional Azeri culture. Elaborate formations such as undulations, bifurcations, folds, and inflections modify this plaza surface into an architectural landscape that performs a multitude of functions: welcoming, embracing, and directing visitors through different levels of the interior. With this gesture, the building blurs the conventional differentiation between architectural object and urban landscape, building envelope and urban plaza, figure and ground, interior and exterior.

Fluidity in architecture is not new to this region. In historical Islamic architecture, rows, grids, or sequences of columns flow to infinity like trees in a forest, establishing nonhierarchical space. Continuous calligraphic and ornamental patterns flow from carpets to walls, walls to ceilings, ceilings to domes, establishing seamless relationships and blurring distinctions between architectural elements and the ground they inhabit. Our intention was to relate to that continuum, not through the use of mimicry or a limiting adherence to the iconography of the past, but rather by developing a firmly contemporary interpretation, reflecting a more nuanced understanding.

Responding to the topographic sheer drop that formerly split the site in two, the project introduces a precisely terraced landscape that establishes alternative connections and routes between public plaza, building, and underground parking. This solution avoids additional excavation and landfill, and successfully converts an initial disadvantage of the site into a key design feature.

GEOMETRY, STRUCTURE, MATERIALITY

One of the most critical yet challenging elements of the project was the architectural development of the building's skin. Our ambition to achieve a surface so continuous that it appears homogeneous, required a broad range of different functions, construction logics, and technical systems to be brought together and integrated into the building's envelope. Advanced computing allowed for the continuous control and communication of these complexities among the numerous project participants.

The Heydar Aliyev Center principally consists of two collaborating systems: a concrete structure combined with a space frame system. In order to achieve large-scale column-free spaces that allow the visitor to experience the fluidity of the interior, vertical structural elements are absorbed by the envelope and curtain wall system. The particular surface geometry fosters unconventional structural solutions, such as the introduction of curved "boot columns" to achieve the inverse peel of the surface from the ground to the west of the building, and the "dovetail" tapering of the cantilever beams that support the building envelope to the east of the site.

The space frame system enabled the construction of a free-form structure and saved significant time throughout the construction process, while the substructure was developed to incorporate a flexible relationship between the rigid grid of the space frame and the free-formed exterior cladding seams. These seams were derived from a process of rationalizing the complex geometry, usage, and aesthetics of the project. Glass Fibre Reinforced Concrete (GFRC) and Glass Fibre Reinforced Polyester (GFRP) were chosen as ideal cladding materials, as they allow for the powerful plasticity of the building's design while responding to very different functional demands related to a variety of situations: plaza, transitional zones, and envelope.

In this architectural composition, if the surface is the music, then the seams between the panels are the rhythm. Numerous studies were carried out on the surface geometry to rationalize the panels while maintaining continuity throughout the building and landscape. The seams promote a greater understanding of the project's scale. They emphasize the continual transformation and implied motion of its fluid geometry, offering a pragmatic solution to practical construction issues such as manufacturing, handling, transportation, and assembly; and answering technical concerns such as accommodating movement due to deflection, external loads, temperature change, seismic activity, and wind loading. To emphasize the continuous relationship between the building's exterior and interior, the lighting of the Heydar Aliyev Center has been very carefully considered. The lighting design strategy differentiates the day and night reading of the building. During the day, the building's volume reflects light, constantly altering the Center's appearance according to the time of day and viewing perspective. The use of semireflective glass gives tantalizing glimpses within, arousing curiosity without revealing the fluid trajectory of spaces inside. At night, this character is gradually transformed by means of lighting that washes from the interior onto the exterior surfaces, unfolding the formal composition to reveal its content and maintaining the fluidity between interior and exterior.

As with all of our work, the Heydar Aliyev Center's design evolved from our investigations and research of the site's topography and the Center's role within its broader cultural landscape. By employing these articulate contextual relationships, the design is embedded within this context, unfolding the future cultural possibilities for the nation.

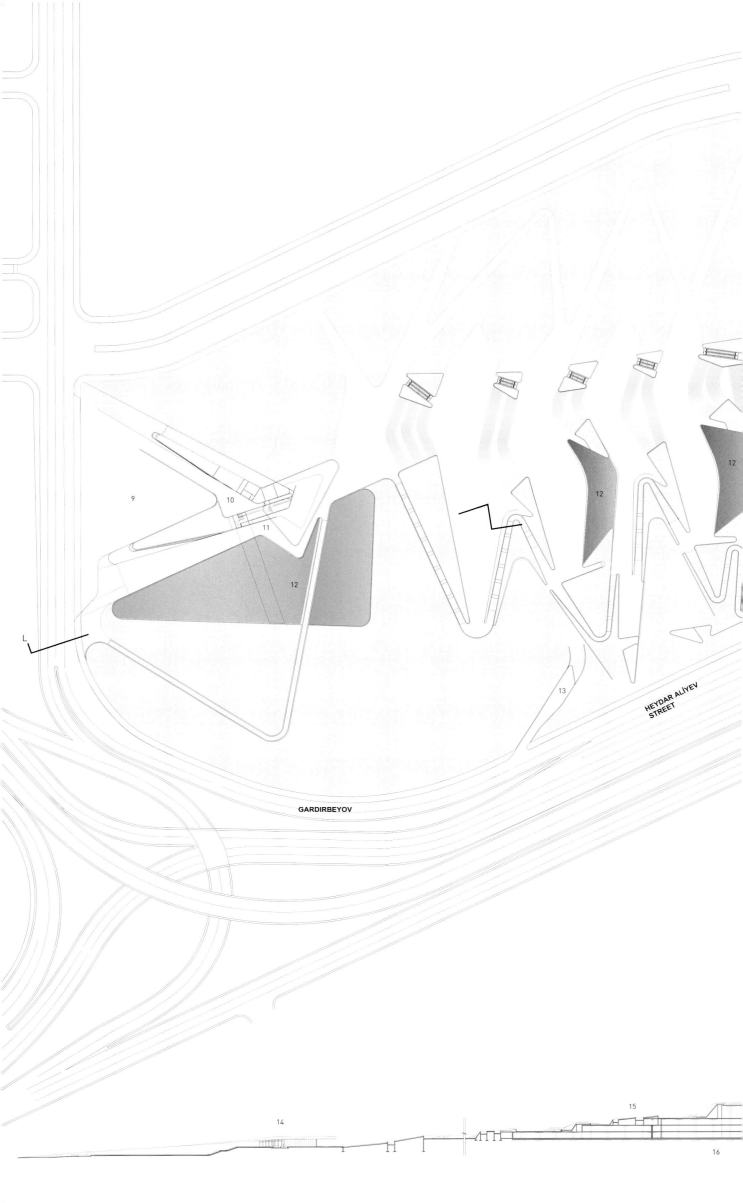

9

10

11

12

L

12

13

12

12

HEYDAR ALİYEV
STREET

GARDIRBEYOV

14

15

16

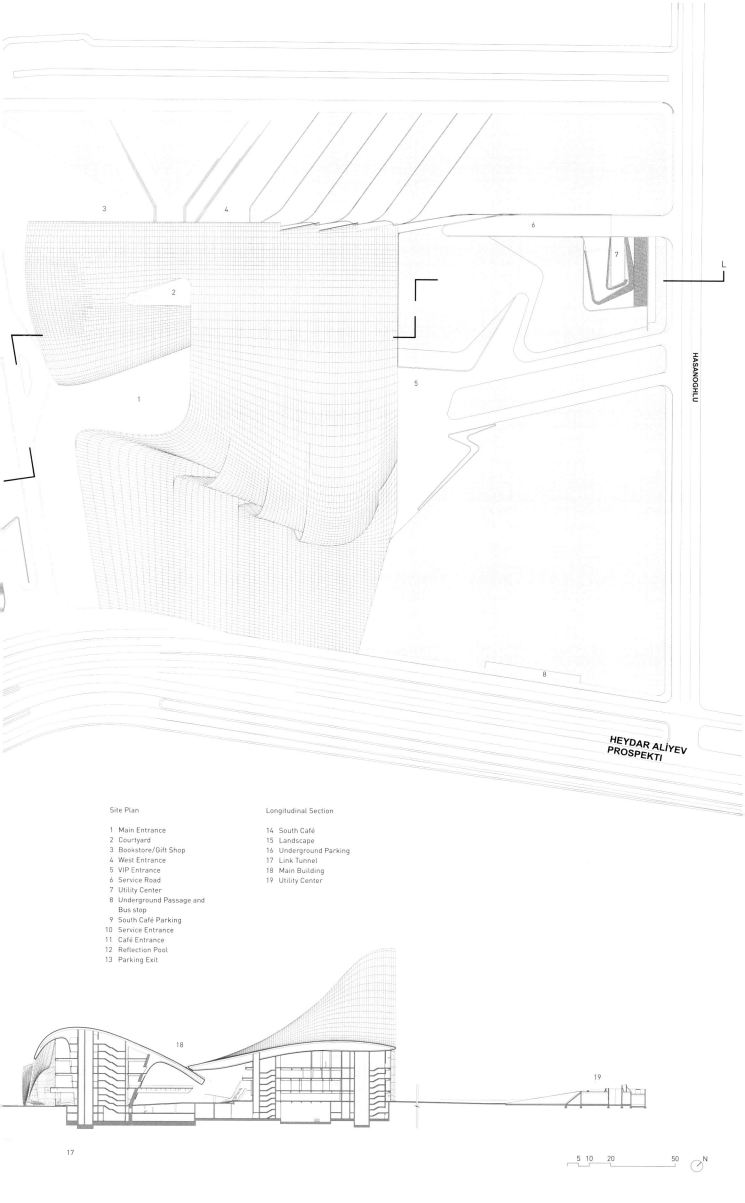

HASANOGHLU

HEYDAR ALİYEV
PROSPEKTI

Site Plan

1 Main Entrance
2 Courtyard
3 Bookstore/Gift Shop
4 West Entrance
5 VIP Entrance
6 Service Road
7 Utility Center
8 Underground Passage and
   Bus stop
9 South Café Parking
10 Service Entrance
11 Café Entrance
12 Reflection Pool
13 Parking Exit

Longitudinal Section

14 South Café
15 Landscape
16 Underground Parking
17 Link Tunnel
18 Main Building
19 Utility Center

5 10 20   50   N

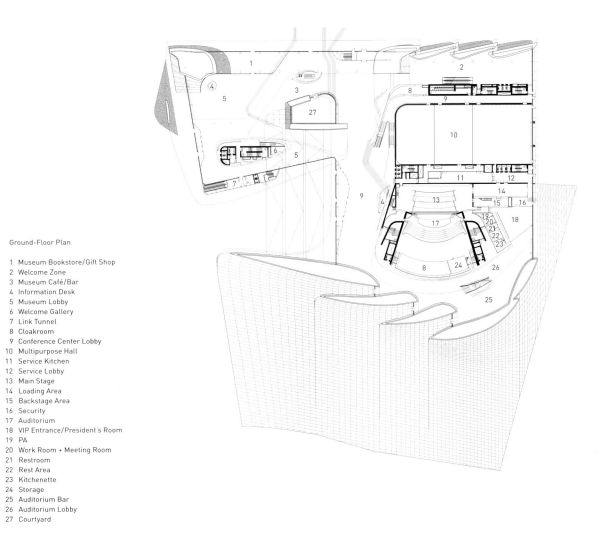

Ground-Floor Plan

1 Museum Bookstore/Gift Shop
2 Welcome Zone
3 Museum Café/Bar
4 Information Desk
5 Museum Lobby
6 Welcome Gallery
7 Link Tunnel
8 Cloakroom
9 Conference Center Lobby
10 Multipurpose Hall
11 Service Kitchen
12 Service Lobby
13 Main Stage
14 Loading Area
15 Backstage Area
16 Security
17 Auditorium
18 VIP Entrance/President's Room
19 PA
20 Work Room + Meeting Room
21 Restroom
22 Rest Area
23 Kitchenette
24 Storage
25 Auditorium Bar
26 Auditorium Lobby
27 Courtyard

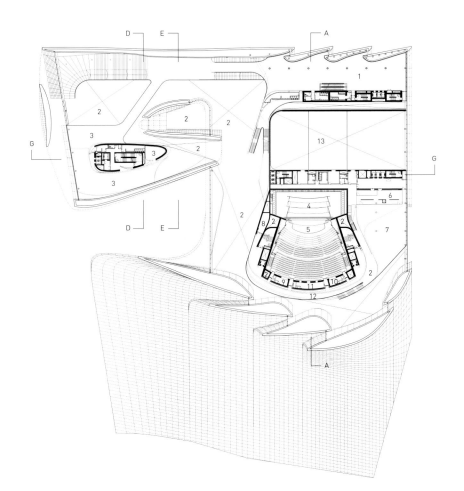

1st-Floor Plan

1 Library
2 Open to Below
3 Thematic Temporary Art Gallery
4 Main Stage
5 Auditorium
6 Service Kitchen
7 Restaurant
8 Storage
9 Lighting Control
10 Sound Control
11 Projection Room
12 Auditorium Balcony
13 Multipurpose Hall/Open to Below

5 10   20   50

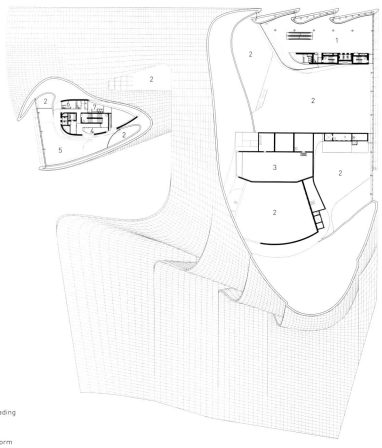

4th-Floor Plan

1 Library Learning and Reading
   Zone
2 Open to Below
3 Stage System Steel Platform
4 Storage
5 Permanent Art Gallery
6 Male Restroom
7 Female Restroom

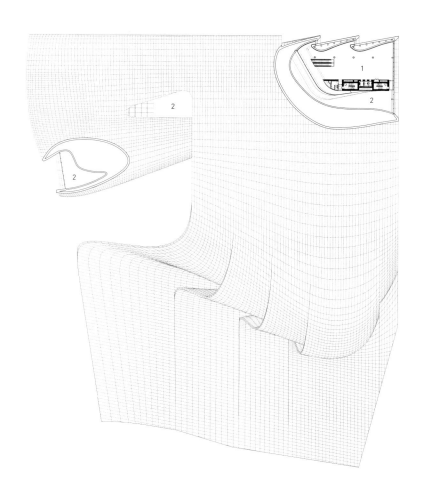

6th-Floor Plan

1 Library
2 Open to Below

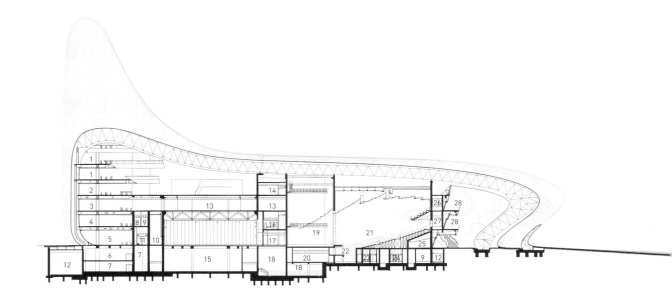

Section A-A

1 Learning and Reading Zone
2 Multimedia Zone
3 Business Zone
4 Children's Activity Zone
5 Welcome Zone
6 Library Storage
7 Library Stack
8 Disabled Restroom
9 Janitor's Room
10 Conference Center Lobby
11 Female Restroom
12 Loading Bay
13 Meeting Room
14 Network Room

15 Auditorium/Multipurpose Hall
     Storage
16 Male Restroom
17 Service Kitchen
18 AHU Room
19 Main Stage
20 Backstage Storage
21 Auditorium
22 Orchestra Pit
23 Guest Dressing Room
24 Women's Locker Room/WC
25 Cloakroom
26 Translator Room
27 Projection Room
28 Balcony

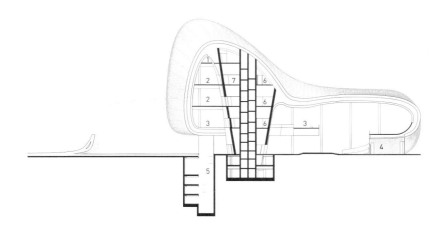

Section D-D

1 President's Suite
2 Permanent Collection Gallery
3 Temporary Exhibition Gallery
4 Museum Bookstore/Gift Shop
5 Passenger Elevator
6 Restroom
7 Storage

5 10   20   50

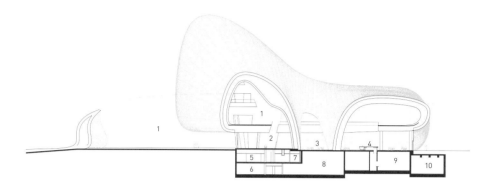

Section E-E

1 Temporary Collection Gallery
2 Museum Lobby
3 Courtyard
4 Museum Café
5 Cloakroom
6 Registration & Art Handling
7 Restroom
8 AHU Room
9 Café Kitchen
10 Loading Bay

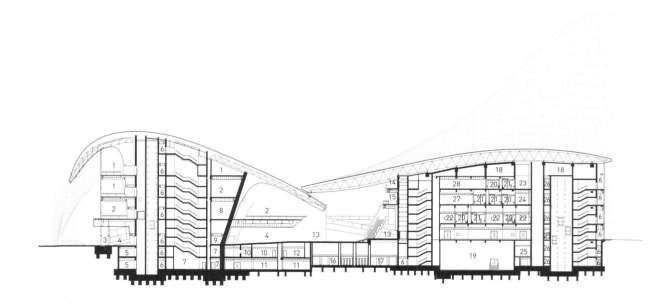

Section G-G

1 Permanent Collection Gallery
2 Temporary Exhibition Gallery
3 Security Vestibule
4 Museum Lobby
5 President/VIP Lobby
6 Vestibule
7 Storage
8 Small Temp Gallery/Dark Room
9 Welcome Gallery
10 Cloakroom
11 Registration + Art Handling
12 Medical Room
13 Conference Center Lobby
14 Organizer's office

15 Meeting Room Lobby
16 Men's Shower/Locker Room
17 Women's Shower/Locker Room
18 Fan Room
19 AHU Room
20 Male Restroom
21 Female Restroom
22 Control Room
23 Admin Offices
24 Mezzanine Café
25 Service Lobby
26 Janitor Room
27 Meeting Room
28 Network Room
29 Disabled Room

CONSTRUCTION, INNOVATION, AND PRINCIPLES

Felix Mara

Many of England's best architectural practices pride themselves on their functionalist, engineering-driven design methodologies. Zaha Hadid Architects' buildings are distinguished by the inventiveness and quality of their construction, but clearly come from a different stable. Though undeniably technically accomplished and the outcome of sophisticated digital design, they are first and foremost works of art; while the practice's output maturely accepts that the artifacts of the construction industry are the medium architects work in, it refuses to allow them, or the orthodoxies and taboos surrounding their use, to cramp its style. Despite design/build procurement, Zaha Hadid Architects expected consultants and specialist contractors working on the Heydar Aliyev Center to dutifully sharpen their pencils and work to the exacting standards it set, rather than habitually sucking air through their teeth and merely paying lip service to the "design intent."

The project team faced high wind loads, large seismic forces, and poor subsoil conditions, but compared to the demands of the architects' proposals and the brief, these were technicalities, especially with a generous budget and cooperative spirit. These proposals involved large spans; precisely defined, smooth double-curvature surfaces in remote locations; and high-quality homogeneous finishes.

But was all this necessity the mother of invention, not to say innovation? There was of course no dearth of formal inventiveness in the architects' camp. The building's external skin and the contiguous undulating surfaces of the surrounding plaza are like a quilted parka, with a smart, directional hierarchy of seams whose dominant contours race and twist across the landscape, and whose light glows through bifurcations in its flanks like a basking shark's gill rakes. But these moves had to be matched by resourcefulness and innovation at the construction coal face. The process of rationalization began with the architects' modeling of the project and the panelization of its envelope. Documentation of this, and the swirling geometry of the auditorium, removed uncertainty about the design objectives.

Much of this energy was directed at the usual aims of accelerating construction and reducing costs, for example by adopting space frame technology for the external shell and lightweight fiberglass reinforced plastic for its outer cladding—spawning secondary challenges, as this had to match the concrete panels surfacing the piazza. The scale and complexity of panel production was epic; installation was accelerated by microchips attached to each unit. There was also great ingenuity in the design of the building shell support structure, which had to make the transition from the angular space frame to the smooth undulations of its cladding, allowing installers to finely calibrate fixing positions.

Highlighting pure innovation is a philatelist's game, and many of the project's construction highlights are better described as expertise: the variable air volume system, which adapts to its range of accommodation; the use of the external envelope as a supply air plenum to avoid louvers in the cladding, which would have compromised the architects' vision; coupled room acoustics, which allow the auditorium to accommodate various activities without adaptation; high coefficient of performance chillers; adaptor frames in the glazing; a space frame grasping at elusive support points... But for pure innovation, look instead at the leitmotif grooves and joints at radiused floor-to-wall junctions whose diminishing depth sends out tactile signals, or Sanset İkoor's fusion of digital technology and craftsmanship to fabricate the layers of timber strips which line the auditorium, or the unitized weathering deck attached to the space frame with waterproofing, insulation, and vapor-control layer preassembled at ground level before being craned into the treacherous working environment above.

One principle alone dominated the many subprinciples of best practice construction and engineering in the making of the Heydar Aliyev Center: the architects' vision is paramount, and all activity is subservient to this. So it's a story of architectural inventiveness matched by the resourcefulness and innovation of consultants and contractors: a marriage made in heaven and formalized in Baku.

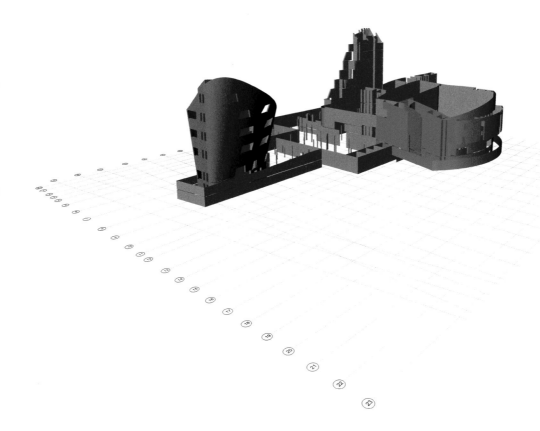

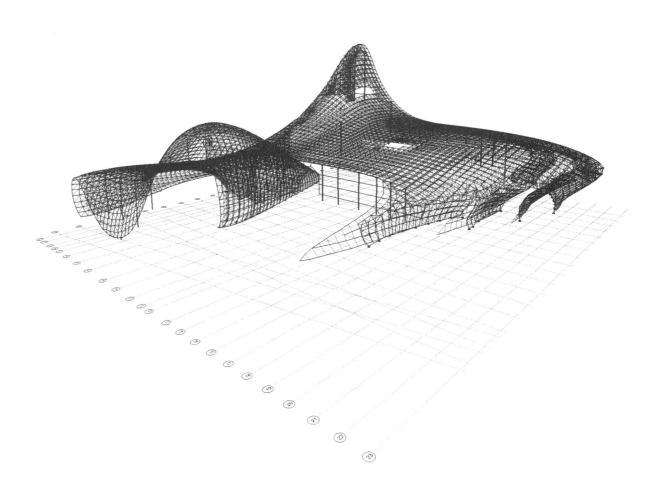

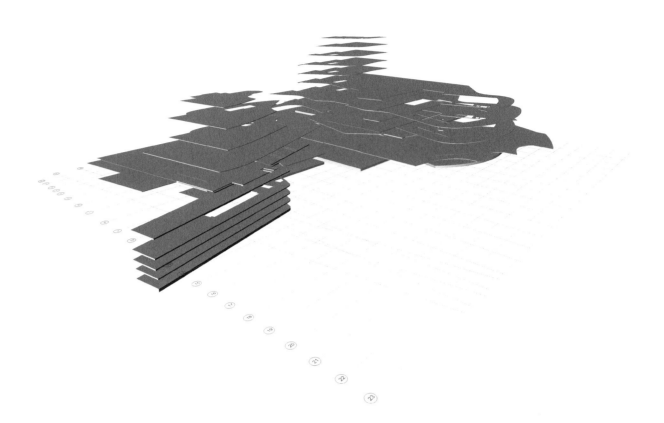

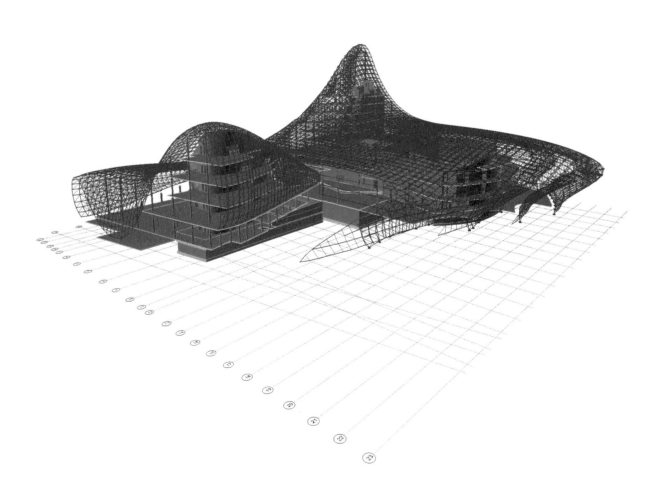

107

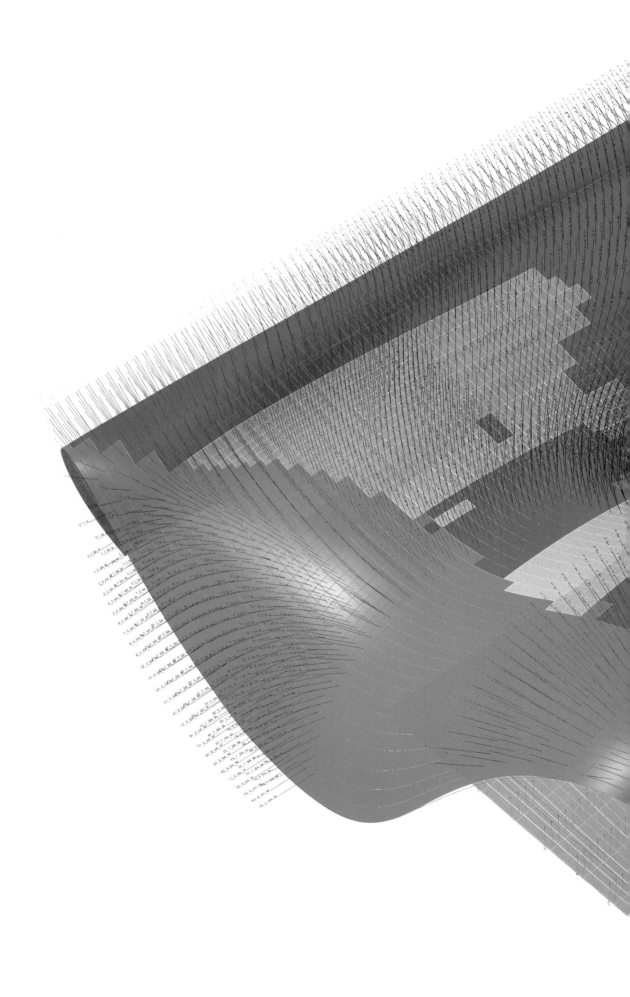

Surface geometry panelization analysis:
double-curvature vs. single-curvature vs. flat panels

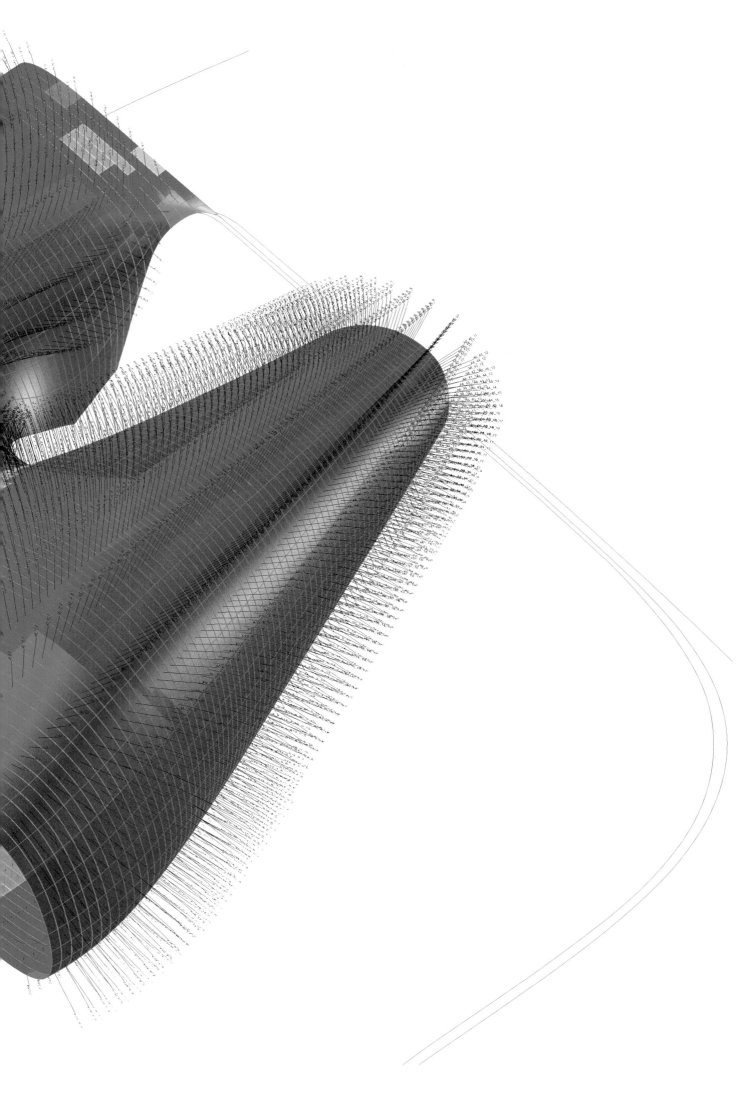

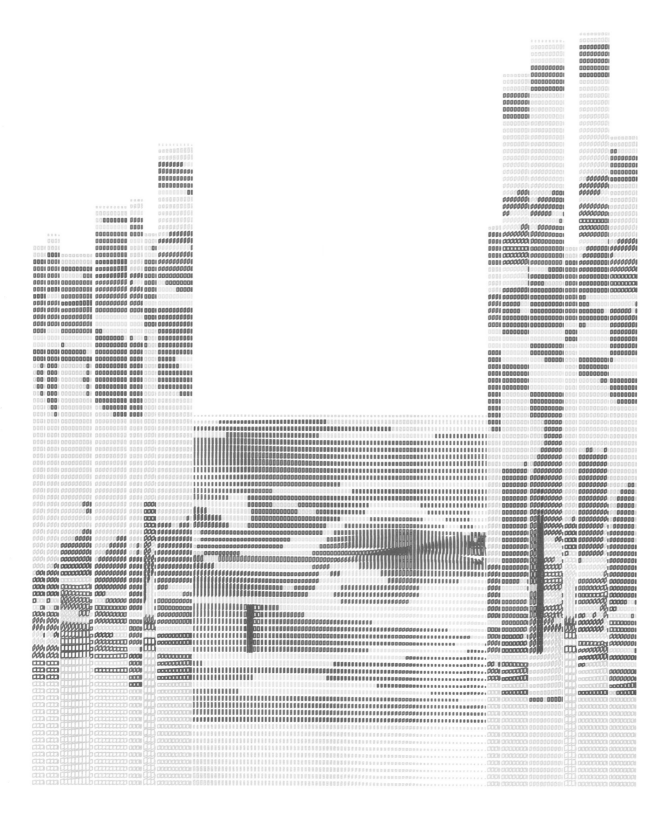

Panelization analysis flattened

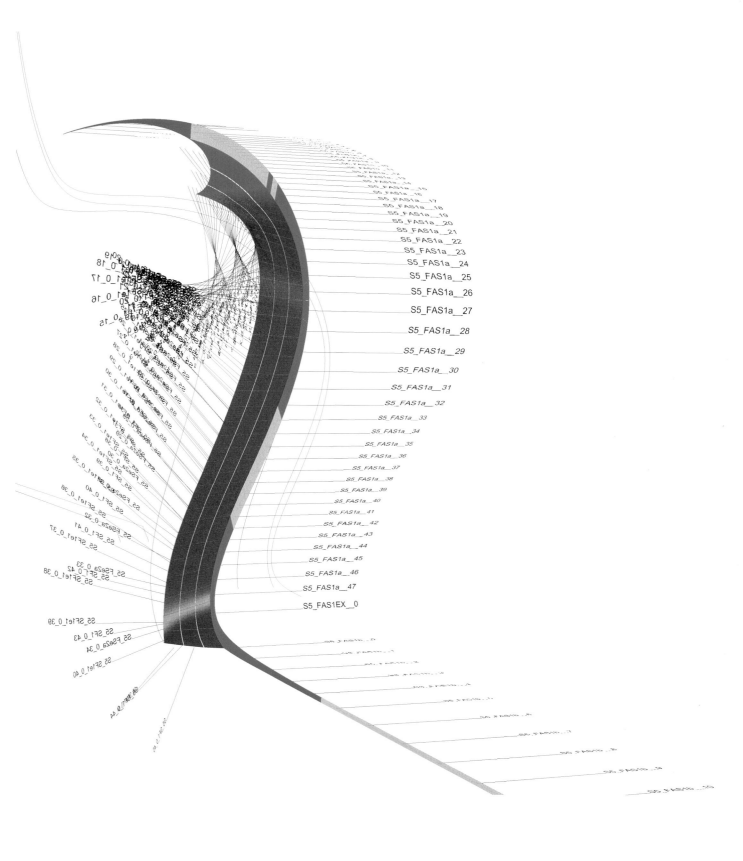

S5_FAS1a__17
S5_FAS1a__18
S5_FAS1a__19
S5_FAS1a__20
S5_FAS1a__21
S5_FAS1a__22
S5_FAS1a__23
S5_FAS1a__24
S5_FAS1a__25
S5_FAS1a__26
S5_FAS1a__27
S5_FAS1a__28
S5_FAS1a__29
S5_FAS1a__30
S5_FAS1a__31
S5_FAS1a__32
S5_FAS1a__33
S5_FAS1a__34
S5_FAS1a__35
S5_FAS1a__36
S5_FAS1a__37
S5_FAS1a__38
S5_FAS1a__39
S5_FAS1a__40
S5_FAS1a__41
S5_FAS1a__42
S5_FAS1a__43
S5_FAS1a__44
S5_FAS1a__45
S5_FAS1a__46
S5_FAS1a__47
S5_FAS1EX__0

WORKING WITH ZAHA HADID ARCHITECTS

Hassan Gozal and Murat Cecen, Founders, DiA Holding

DiA Holding has been privileged to contribute to several important architectural projects in Azerbaijan's capital, Baku, as the city rapidly gains prominence on the world stage. Working with Zaha Hadid Architects to realize the Heydar Aliyev Center has been one of the greatest pleasures, and greatest challenges, of our work in Azerbaijan thus far.

Cultural projects represent some of the most exciting opportunities for innovation and experimentation in contemporary architecture, and yet they also command the highest levels of respect and responsibility for those tasked with building them. To create public space—whether a museum, art gallery or opera house—is to contribute to the very soul of a city; to weave together its culture and people in the collective dialogue that is such a vital component of a rich urban life and cityscape.

Zaha Hadid Architects' design for the Heydar Aliyev Center set out to do just this. With unmatched ambition, their design would not simply occupy a site within the landscape of Baku, but instead, its fluid geometries would become an integral part of the urbanism of the city itself; an essential forum for the exchange of ideas.

The context of Hadid's work demands our consideration. It is uplifting and purposeful, celebrating the complexity and fluidity of natural systems; a persuasive manifesto of nature's logic and unity. When the Heydar Aliyev Foundation enthusiastically embraced Zaha Hadid Architects' proposal in 2007, DiA Holding was tasked with realizing this remarkable building.

The Heydar Aliyev Center brings together diverse disciplines in a single, holistic entity. Similarly, the process of constructing the building was also an exercise in intense collaboration. DiA Holding was not only the main contractor for the project, but also served as the executive architect and project manager; bringing together a wide range of regional and international subcontractors and consultants to construct the building.

Throughout history, a tenet of truly great architecture is the application of technological advances to create magnificent, inspirational spaces. Innovative design has always driven the development of new technologies and construction techniques, and DiA is proud to be part of this process, delivering solutions that have enabled Zaha Hadid Architects to deliver their spectacular vision.

The Heydar Aliyev Center commanded precise engineering and expertise in complex construction technologies at the highest standards, and DiA assembled a team of world-leading consultants and subcontractors to complete the project. Where solutions were not readily found, we established an enviable record of invention through rigorous research and experimentation. DiA wholeheartedly embraced these challenges, with an unwavering dedication to upholding the integrity of Zaha Hadid Architects' unique design. It is a testament to the skill, passion, and professionalism of the team.

When we began this journey with Zaha Hadid Architects we, and our collaborators, were beyond our comfort zone. How would we realize such an ambitious vision? It was an immense challenge with a steep learning curve for all parties. Ultimately this experience, this very process of guiding the vision and watching it emerge from the ground, has enhanced our belief that continually pushing the boundaries of possibility can achieve the most exceptional results.

The Heydar Aliyev Center is many things: a triumph of contemporary design and construction; a symbol of Baku's rich cultural history and the promising future of Azerbaijan; a shining example of what can result from such enlightened patronage. It is a testament to what can be achieved when we put aside our preconceived notions of what is possible and commit to working together in the purest spirit of collaboration, to make manifest an extraordinary vision.

JOSEPH GIOVANNINI is an architecture critic and architect based in New York. He holds degrees from Yale and Harvard universities, and has taught at Columbia University, Harvard, UCLA, USC, the Southern California Institute of Architects, and most recently at the Pratt Institute in New York. He has written for the *New York Times, New York Magazine, Architect Magazine, Architectural Record,* the *Los Angeles Herald Examiner,* and many other publications, and was nominated for a Pulitzer Prize in criticism.

ZAHA HADID ARCHITECTS
Zaha Hadid, founder of Zaha Hadid Architects, was awarded the Pritzker Architecture Prize (considered to be the Nobel Prize of architecture) in 2004 and is internationally known for her built, theoretical and academic work. Each of her dynamic and pioneering projects builds on more than thirty years of exploration and research in the interrelated fields of urbanism, architecture, and design.

Born in Baghdad, Iraq, in 1950, Hadid studied mathematics at the American University of Beirut before moving to London in 1972 to attend the Architectural Association (AA) School, where she was awarded the Diploma Prize in 1977. She founded Zaha Hadid Architects in 1979 and completed her first building, the Vitra Fire Station, Germany, in 1993.

Hadid taught at the AA School until 1987 and has since held numerous chairs and guest professorships at universities around the world. She is currently a professor at the University of Applied Arts in Vienna and visiting professor of Architectural Design at Yale University.

Working with senior office partner, Patrik Schumacher, Hadid's interest lies in the rigorous interface between architecture, landscape, and geology as her practice integrates natural topography and human-made systems, leading to innovation with new technologies.

Zaha Hadid Architects continues to be a global leader in pioneering research and design investigation. Collaborations with corporations that lead their industries have advanced the practice's diversity and knowledge, while the implementation of state-of-the-art technologies have aided the realization of fluid and therefore complex architectural structures.
www.zaha-hadid.com

ARCHITECT
Zaha Hadid Architects

DESIGN
Zaha Hadid, Patrik Schumacher

PROJECT DESIGNER AND ARCHITECT
Saffet Kaya Bekiroglu

PROJECT TEAM
Sara Sheikh Akbari
Shiqi Li
Phil Soo Kim
Marc Boles
Yelda Gin
Liat Muller
Deniz Manisali
Lillie Liu
Jose Lemos
Simone Fuchs
Jose Ramon Tramoyeres
Yu Du
Tahmina Parvin
Erhan Patat
Fadi Mansour
Jaime Bartolome
Josef Glas
Michael Grau
Deepti Zachariah
Ceyhun Baskin
Daniel Widrig
Murat Mutlu

Special thanks to Charles Walker

MAIN CONTRACTOR AND ARCHITECT OF RECORD
DiA Holding

CONSULTANTS
Tuncel Engineering, AKT (Structure)
GMD Project (Mechanical)
HB Engineering (Electrical)
Werner Sobek (Façade)
Etik Fire Consultancy (Fire)
Mezzo Stüdyo (Acouctic)
Enar Engineering (Geotechnical)
Sigal (Infrastructure)
MBLD (Lighting)

SUBCONTRACTORS AND MANUFACTURERS
MERO (Steel Space Frame System) + Bilim Makina (Installation
of Space Frame System)
Doka (Formwork)
Arabian Profile (External Cladding Panels/GRC & GRP)
Lindner (Internal Skin Cladding)
Sanset İkoor (Auditorium Wooden Cladding)
Quinette (Auditorium Seats)
Zumtobel (Lighting Fixtures)
Baswa (Special Acoustic Ceilings) + Astas (Installation of Ceilings)
Solarlux (Multipurpose Hall Façade Door)
Bolidt (Polyurethane Floor Finish)
Kone Elevators + Ikma (Installation of Elevators)
MM Mühendisler Mermer (Marble Cladding Works)
HRN Dizayn (Landscape LED Installation)
Thyssen Group (Escalator)
Remak Makina (Fire Doors and Concrete-Cladded Doors)
Tema (Gypsum Panel Works)
MIM Mühendislik (Structural Steel)
Elekon Enerji Sistemleri (Main Building Lighting Control System)
NIS Epoksi Kaplama Sistemleri (Epoxy Works)
Light Projects Group (Lighting Fixtures)
Limit İnşaat (External Skin Insulations and Structure)

ZAHA HADID ARCHITECTS
HEYDAR ALIYEV CENTER

Edited by Saffet Kaya Bekiroglu

Concept: Saffet Kaya Bekiroglu, Lars Müller
Editorial team: Roger Howie, Marlon Rueberg, Chantelle Lue Elton
Design: Lars Müller and Saffet Kaya Bekiroglu with Integral Lars Müller
Copyediting: Zaha Hadid Architects
Proofreading: Keonaona Peterson
Lithography: Ast & Fischer, Wabern, Switzerland
Printing and binding: Kösel, Altusried-Krugzell, Germany
Debossing die: Pro Gravur AG, Bern, Switzerland
Paper: Allegro 150 g/m²

IMAGE CREDITS
Iwan Baan 2–3, 14–15, 24–25, 62–65, 116–17, 120–21, 126–27
Hélène Binet 4–13, 16–21, 26–61, 66–77, 90–91, 96–103, 118–19, 122–23
Courtesy of DiA Holding 22–23, 104–05, 112–13
Luke Hayes 94–95
Courtesy of Sanset İkoor 78–79

Lars Müller Publishers
Zürich, Switzerland
www.lars-mueller-publishers.com

ISBN 978-3-03778-353-5

Printed in Germany